W9-BEJ-995

A Faith to Confess

The
Baptist Confession of Faith
of 1689

Rewritten
in
Modern English

CAREY PUBLICATIONS LTD

COPYRIGHT CAREY PUBLICATIONS 1975

Eighth edition 1997

All rights reserved — no part of this book may be reproduced in any form without permission in writing from the publisher, except by a reviewer who wishes to quote brief passages in connection with a review in magazine or newspaper.

ISBN 0 85479 940 0

Published by Carey Publications Ltd
75 Woodhill Road, Leeds LS16 7BZ

**Printed and bound in Great Britain by
Creative Print and Design (Wales), Ebbw Vale, Gwent**

CONTENTS

INTRODUCTION

A Faith to Confess is designed to present a clear outline of Biblical
truth to all interested persons.   Since the Bible, the fully inspired
Word of God, does not change from one age to another, the
truths contained in the Confession, wholly based as they are upon
Scripture, are as relevant today as when 'the Elders and Brethren
of many congregations of Christians, baptized upon profession
of their Faith' stated them in 1677.   Charles II was then upon the
British throne.   It was a time of persecution.

Between the years 1644 and 1648 an Assembly of Puritan
Divines of England and Scotland had drawn up the Westminster
Confession which was and is highly esteemed by believers.   But
its church Order was that of Presbyterianism, and Baptists
differed from it on important matters such as the nature of the
gathered church, baptism, the Lord's supper and church government.   Hence, when opportunity arose, they drew up their own
Confession of Faith, accepting the fundamental doctrines of the
Westminster Confession but making such adjustments to, and
correction of, that Confession as seemed to their minds and
consciences to be demanded by the pure Word of God.   Thus
a comparison of the two Confessions will reveal many word-for-
word similarities but also sundry changes.

A dozen years after the Baptist Confession was drawn up by
persecuted ministers a new era of liberty dawned, and in 1689
thirty-seven leading Baptist ministers re-issued the Confession.
In England and Wales it became the definitive Confession of the
Particular or Calvinistic churches and remained so for the next
two centuries.   Its alternative title was the Old London Confession.   In 1744 it was adopted by the Calvinistic Baptists of
North America, and called by them the Philadelphia Confession
of Faith.

The youthful C. H. Spurgeon had been minister of the New Park Street Chapel, London, for a few months only when, in 1855, he determined to strengthen the doctrinal foundations of that and other churches by the re-issue of the 1689 Confession. In this way it was given a new lease of life. The twentieth century has also witnessed to its relevance and usefulness, for in 1958 it was again reprinted, with further editions in 1963, 1966, 1970 and 1974. Recent decades have seen a revival of the Reformed Faith, not least among Baptists. The revivifying of old churches and the planting of new churches in various parts of the world has given renewed emphasis to the need for a Confession which sets forth fundamentals of the Faith in clear and concise language.

Carey Publications Limited felt, however, that the Confession of 1689 in its original form presented certain difficulties. An essential of any doctrinal statement is that it should be capable of being clearly understood by those who are invited to use it. As far as possible its language must be that of the time of its issue; ambiguities must be avoided; clarity must be its hallmark. After nearly three hundred years the Confession of William III's reign no longer meets these requirements, and Mr. S. M. Houghton of Charlbury, Oxford, was invited by the Publishers to rewrite the Confession in a modern style, retaining the exact sense of the original—this is guaranteed!—but transposing phrases and changing words, to render the meaning, as far as possible, crystal clear. It is believed that, in this new form, the Confession will have a still greater usefulness wherever the English language is spoken.

Baptist ministers need experience no hesitation in recommending the Confession to their members as a document that maintains doctrinal precision with a reasonable degree of fulness. It is not, of course, to be held as an infallible and authoritative rule. Believers are bound by Scripture, by the whole of Scripture, and by nothing but the Scripture. At the same time, however, it is highly necessary and undeniably useful to have a clear statement in modern language of the Faith we believe and practise and commend to all men.

Those newly converted to the Christian Faith are not expected at the outset either to know or understand all the great doctrines set out in the Confession. But acquaintance with all facets of the Faith is something to be pursued from the moment of conversion, and the more so because there are many winds of false doctrine in the modern world ready to blow young plants out of the ground. The modern idiom will aid young Christians, and the texts to which they are directed will be a guide for them in Bible study. We have not followed the method of inserting, after every other sentence or so, a figure to guide to a Biblical text, but have adopted the more modern practice of giving textual references at the end of the paragraphs. Those who use the Confession are requested to compare the statements made with the texts to which attention is called, but at the same time to remember—and this is a very important matter—that statements in the Confession do not hinge upon any one text, but are keyed to 'the whole counsel of God'.

While it is hoped that all members of churches will steadfastly believe the doctrines of the Confession, it is unlikely that they will all become expert theologians. But the Reformed awakening of today has given renewed thrust to the Biblical teaching concerning Elders, who are, by definition, expected to possess an aptitude to teach and to be able by sound doctrine to exhort and to convince gainsayers (Titus 1:9). Here, then, is a Faith for churches to be founded upon, and a Faith for church officers to teach, defend, and hand on to future generations (1 Tim. 3:15, 16).

We can rightly claim that well-established believers of the Baptist persuasion will find little, if any, difficulty in giving assent to the great truths which are covered by the Confession. Such fundamental doctrines as those of the Trinity, Providence, the Fall of Man, the Atonement, Justification, and Repentance are the common heritage of all who worthily bear the name of Christian. On the other hand, there are matters to which the Confession makes reference which do not command such universal assent, and on which, indeed, opinions are divided. This very fact reminds us that the Confession is not acclaimed as an infallible statement on a par with Scripture. But certainly it expresses in up-to-date language the sum and substance of the ancient Gospel of martyrs, confessors, reformers and saints, and, as Spurgeon said of the Confession when he republished it in 1856, 'It is *the truth of God*, against which the gates of hell shall not prevail'. At the same time, however, readers will find several interpretations which are admittedly disputed at the present day. We call attention to some of them.

(1) *In chapter 26, paragraph 4, the Pope of Rome is declared to be 'the antichrist', 'the man of sin', 'the son of perdition'.*
This view, held by the Reformers and Puritans, is not universally held today, not because believers do not deplore the errors of Romanism (and of modern Protestantism for that matter), but on exegetical grounds. Some Christians are prepared to believe and say that the primary reference of 'the little apocalypse', as 2 Thessalonians 2:2-9 is called, is to the Pope; some speak and write otherwise. The various commentaries show that there are reasonable grounds for proposing alternative interpretations, and, in the absence of unanimity, no attempt can rightly be made to demand an obligatory belief of any one line of interpretation. In the area of prophecy (eschatology) it is particularly needful to be cautious, for only in the consummation of all things will the precise meaning of apocalyptic passages of the Word be made clear. In other words, we are not prepared to claim that the prophetical interpretations made by the Reformers of the sixteenth century and the Puritans of the seventeenth century stand on the same level as their doctrinal affirmations.

(2) *Despite the close alignment of the 1689 Confession with the Westminster Confession, the substance of Chapter 20 is not to be found in the Westminster Confession, but is, with scarcely any*

variation, taken from The Savoy Declaration of Faith and Order, 1658, issued by the Congregational-Independents. Why did the compilers see fit to make this addition? Dr. Jack Milner of Derby has made a study of this question and writes as follows:

When we look at chapter twenty as a whole it seems as if the compilers recognized the need for a definition of the gospel *as sent out into the world.*

The first paragraph contains a statement of the necessity of God's grace followed in the second paragraph by an affirmation of the absolute necessity of gospel preaching, designed to emphasize the fact that the gospel is revealed nowhere but in the Bible. Paragraph three shows that the actual sending of the gospel is in the hands of God. Although the precept of Scripture directs Christians to preach the gospel to every creature, the sovereign will and good pleasure of God alone determine the particular nations and individuals to whom the gospel actually comes. The final paragraph of chapter twenty is a re-affirmation of the doctrine of effectual calling with a reminder that the gospel preacher, in declaring the truth, is fulfilling his duty.

The force of the Great Commission was plainly felt by the compilers and they sought to draw attention to the absolute distinction between 'the church' and 'the world'. Before the days of Constantine the Church could be seen to be a community of people called out of the world. Their separateness was their strength for they were saved from their sin and they called on their fellows to be partakers of the same salvation. In their zeal the believers fulfilled the Great Commission and the Lord added many to their number. Under Constantine, however, Christianity became the official religion of the Empire, having the protection of the State. The distinction between the Church and the world disappeared and a 'church' consisted of everyone in a particular locality and not of a group of people called out of and spiritually separate from the world.

At the time of the Reformation, the conception of the Church which dated from the reign of Constantine and prevailed during the Middle Ages was inherited substantially by the Reformers, most of whom thought in terms of Christian countries, states or cities.

Anabaptists on the Continent saw clearly that the church must be a separate community taken out of the world and thus the Reformers became their bitter enemies, calling them 'purists' and 'perfectionists'.

In the seventeenth century the Presbyterians who compiled the Westminster Confession still believed in Christianity in a territorial sense and so they still thought of the church as being supported by the magistrate. Only gradually did the Baptists begin to oppose the idea of a state church with its mixture of believers and unbelievers, and to see themselves as a gathered-out community. Gradually they began to have a view of themselves in their relationship with the world which led them to reject the whole idea of the church being linked in Presbyterian or Anglican fashion with the State. This progress towards a correct view of the church in the world is the distinctive feature of chapter twenty of the 1689 Confession of Faith.

(3) *It has been suggested that the Confession is out of date and inadequate in respect of the inerrancy of Scripture.*
Forces hostile to the gospel have attacked unceasingly the authority of the Word of God. Obviously the writers of the Confession could not anticipate the controversies of our day. The Confession declares the divine origin, the perfect nature, the absolute authority and the complete sufficiency of the holy Scriptures. In recent times the authority of Scripture has been undermined in a subtle way by what is termed 'the new herme-neutic', the idea that the Scriptures were relevant for the apostolic times but now require new principles of interpretation for our modern epoch. For instance, it is claimed that we are now in a more enlightened era concerning the question of the man/ woman relationship and therefore the prohibitions of 1 Timothy 2:12 and 1 Corinthians 14:34,35 are no longer applicable. In

many other ways the notion of irrelevance can be used to undermine the authority of Scripture. It is important therefore to assert that the Scriptures are timeless in their relevance and application. For example, all the ramifications of the personal fall in time and space of our first parents, Adam and Eve, described in Genesis 3 apply equally now as in any previous age.

A further challenge to the supreme authority of Scripture is the claim that prophecies continue today, prophecies that are a mixture of good and bad and not on a par with the original Scripture. These claims are derogatory in two ways. Firstly to support the claim it is suggested that mixed type prophecy good and bad (only partially reliable) existed in the New Testament, that of Agabus being an example. [Victor Budgen writing in the magazine *Reformation Today* issues 101 and 102 defends the prophecy of Agabus.] Secondly the notion that further prophecy is needed implies the inadequacy of Scripture. It is necessary therefore to emphasise the divine origin of Scripture. All Scripture is God-breathed and therefore wholly free of error and infallible (incapable of teaching error). The divine inspiration of Scripture is plenary, that is it extends to all parts alike. Finally it is needful to assert the unique nature of Scripture as the source of truth and the means by which the Church is to be guided and fed to the end of time, no prophecies of any kind being required to ameliorate or assist the Scriptures in that unique function.

(4) *In the interests of clarity the word 'elect' has been inserted at the opening of paragraph 3 in Chapter 10.*
This is based on three considerations:
(a) Throughout the Confession it is axiomatic that none but 'elect' persons are saved or can be saved.
(b) Except for the word 'elect', paragraph 3 Chapter 10 is taken from the Westminster Confession of 1648, and obviously the addition of the word 'elect' makes no change whatsoever to the meaning of the paragraph.

(c) The use of the expression 'all elect persons' later in the paragraph simply carries further the meaning of the expression 'elect infants'.

CHAPTER 1

THE HOLY SCRIPTURE

1 THE Holy Scripture is the all-sufficient, certain and infallible rule or standard of the knowledge, faith and obedience that constitute salvation. Although the light of nature, and God's works of creation and providence, give such clear testimony to His goodness, wisdom and power that men who spurn them are left inexcusable, yet they are not sufficient of themselves to give that knowledge of God and His will which is necessary for salvation. In consequence the merciful Lord from time to time and in a variety of ways has revealed Himself, and made known His will to His church. And furthermore, in order to ensure the preservation and propagation of the truth, and the establishment and comfort of the church against the corrupt nature of man and the malice of Satan and the world, He caused this revelation of Himself and His will to be written down in all its fulness. And as the manner in which God formerly revealed His will has long ceased, the Holy Scripture becomes absolutely essential to men.

Ps. 19:1-3; Prov. 22:19-21; Isa. 8:20; Luke 16:29,31; Rom. 1:19-21; 2:14, 15; 15:4; Eph. 2:20; 2 Tim. 3:15-17; Heb. 1:1; 2 Pet. 1:19,20.

2 The Holy Scripture, or the Word of God written, consists of the following books which together make up the Old and New Testaments:

THE OLD TESTAMENT

Genesis	1 Kings	Ecclesiastes	Amos
Exodus	2 Kings	Song of Solomon	Obadiah
Leviticus	1 Chronicles	(or Canticles)	Jonah
Numbers	2 Chronicles	Isaiah	Micah
Deuteronomy	Ezra	Jeremiah	Nahum
Joshua	Nehemiah	Lamentations	Habakkuk
Judges	Esther	Ezekiel	Zephaniah
Ruth	Job	Daniel	Haggai
1 Samuel	Psalms	Hosea	Zechariah
2 Samuel	Proverbs	Joel	Malachi

THE NEW TESTAMENT

Matthew	Ephesians	James
Mark	Philippians	1 Peter
Luke	Colossians	2 Peter
John	1 Thessalonians	1 John
Acts of the	2 Thessalonians	2 John
Apostles	1 Timothy	3 John
Romans	2 Timothy	Jude
1 Corinthians	Titus	Revelation
2 Corinthians	Philemon	
Galatians	Hebrews	

All these books are given by the inspiration of God to be the rule or standard of faith and life.

2 Tim. 3:16.

3   The books commonly called the Apocrypha were not given by divine inspiration and are not part of the canon or rule of Scripture.   Therefore they do not possess any authority in the church of God, and are to be regarded and used in the same way as other writings of men.

Luke 24:27,44; Rom. 3:2.

4   The Scripture is self-authenticating.   Its authority does not depend upon the testimony of any man or church, but entirely upon God, its author, who is truth itself.   It is to be received because it is the Word of God.

1 Thess. 2:13; 2 Tim. 3:16; 2 Pet. 1:19-21; 1 John 5:9.

5   The testimony of the church of God may influence and persuade us to hold the Scripture in the highest esteem.   The heavenliness of its contents, the efficacy of its doctrine, the majesty of its style, the agreement between all its parts from first to last, the fact that throughout it gives all glory to God, the full revelation it gives of the only way of salvation—these, together with many other incomparably high qualities and full perfections, supply abundant evidence that it is the Word of God.   At the same time, however, we recognize that our full persuasion and assurance of its infallible truth and divine authority is the outcome

of the inward work of the Holy Spirit bearing witness by and with the Word in our hearts.

John 16:13,14; 1 Cor. 2:10-12; 1 John 2:20,27.

6 The sum total of God's revelation concerning all things essential to His own glory, and to the salvation and faith and life of men, is either explicitly set down or implicitly contained in the Holy Scripture. Nothing, whether a supposed revelation of the Spirit or man's traditions, is ever to be added to Scripture.

At the same time, however, we acknowledge that inward enlightenment from the Spirit of God is necessary for the right understanding of what Scripture reveals. We also accept that certain aspects of the worship of God and of church government, which are matters of common usage, are to be determined by the light of nature and Christian common sense, in line with the general rules of God's Word from which there must be no departure.

John 6:45; 1 Cor. 2:9-12; 11:13,14; 14:26,40; Gal. 1:8,9; 2 Tim. 3:15-17.

7 The contents of the Scripture vary in their degree of clarity, and some men have a better understanding of them than others. Yet those things which are essential to man's salvation and which must be known, believed and obeyed, are so clearly propounded and explained in one place or another, that men educated or uneducated may attain to a sufficient understanding of them if they but use the ordinary means.

Ps. 19:7; 119:130; 2 Pet. 3:16.

8 The Old Testament in Hebrew and the New Testament in Greek (that is to say, in their original languages before translation) were inspired by God at first hand, and ever since, by His particular care and providence, they have been kept pure. They are therefore authentic and, for the church, constitute the final court of appeal in all religious controversies. All God's people have a right to, and an interest in, the Scripture, and they are commanded in the fear of God to read and search it. But as the Hebrew and Greek are not known to all such readers, Scrip-

ture is to be translated into every human language, so that as men thus acquire knowledge of God they may worship Him in an acceptable manner, and 'through patience and comfort of the Scriptures may have hope'.

Isa. 8:20; John 5:39; Acts 15:15; Rom. 3:2; 1 Cor. 14:6,9,11,12,24,28; Col. 3:16; Rom. 15:4.

9 It is an infallible rule that Scripture is to be interpreted by Scripture, that is to say, one part by another. Hence any dispute as to the true, full and evident meaning of a particular passage must be determined in the light of clearer, comparable passages.

Acts 15:15,16; 2 Pet. 1:20-21.

10 All religious controversies are to be settled by Scripture, and by Scripture alone. All decrees of Councils, opinions of ancient writers, and doctrines of men collectively or individually, are similarly to be accepted or rejected according to the verdict of the Scripture given to us by the Holy Spirit. In that verdict faith finds its final rest.

Matt. 22:29,31,32; Acts 28:23; Eph. 2:20.

CHAPTER 2

GOD AND THE HOLY TRINITY

1 THERE is but one, and only one, living and true God. He is self-existent and infinite in His being and His perfections. None but He can comprehend or understand His essence. He is pure spirit, invisible, and without body, parts, or the changeable feelings of men. He alone possesses immortality, and dwells amid the light insufferably bright to mortal men. He never changes. He is great beyond all our conceptions, eternal, incomprehensible, almighty and infinite. He is most holy, wise,

free and absolute. All that He does is the out-working of His changeless, righteous will, and for His own glory. He is most loving, gracious, merciful and compassionate. He abounds in goodness and truth. He forgives iniquity, transgression and sin. He rewards those who seek Him diligently. But He hates sin. He will not overlook guilt or spare the guilty, and He is perfectly just in executing judgment.

Gen. 17:1; Exod. 3:14; 34:6,7; Deut. 4:15,16; 6:4; 1 Kings 8:27; Neh. 9: 32,33; Ps. 5:5,6; 90:2; 115:3; Prov. 16:4; Isa. 6:3; 46:10; 48:12; Jer. 10:10; 23:23,24; Nah. 1:2,3; Mal. 3:6; John 4:24; Rom. 11:36; 1 Cor. 8:4,6; 1 Tim. 1:17; Heb. 11:6.

2 God is all-sufficient, and all life, glory, goodness and blessedness are found in Him and in Him alone. He does not stand in need of any of the creatures that He has made, nor does He derive any part of His glory from them. On the contrary, He manifests His own glory in and by them. He is the fountain-head of all being, and the origin, channel and end of all things. Over all His creatures He is sovereign. He uses them as He pleases, and does for them or to them all that He wills. His sight penetrates to the heart of all things. His knowledge is infinite and infallible. No single thing is to Him at risk or uncertain, for He is not dependent upon created things. In all His decisions, doings and demands He is most holy. Angels and men owe to Him as their creator all worship, service and obedience, and whatever else He may require at their hands.

Job 22:2,3; Ps. 119:68; 145:17; 148:13; Ezek. 11:5; Dan. 4:25,34,35; John 5:26; Acts 15:18; Rom. 11:34-36; Heb. 4:13; Rev. 5:12-14.

3 Three divine Persons constitute the Godhead—the Father, the Son (or the Word), and the Holy Spirit. They are one in substance, in power, and in eternity. Each is fully God, and yet the Godhead is one and indivisible. The Father owes His being to none. He is Father to the Son who is eternally begotten of Him. The Holy Spirit proceeds from the Father and the Son. These Persons, one infinite and eternal God not to be divided in nature or in being, are distinguished in Scripture by their personal

relations within the Godhead, and by the variety of works which they undertake. Their tri-unity (that is, the doctrine of the Trinity) is the essential basis of all our fellowship with God, and of the comfort we derive from our dependence upon Him.

Exod. 3:14; Matt. 28:19; John 1:14,18; 14:11; 15:26; 1 Cor. 8:6; 2 Cor. 13:14; Gal. 4:6; 1 John 5:7.

CHAPTER 3

GOD'S DECREE

1 FROM all eternity God decreed all that should happen in time, and this He did freely and unalterably, consulting only His own wise and holy will. Yet in so doing He does not become in any sense the author of sin, nor does He share responsibility for sin with sinners. Neither, by reason of His decree, is the will of any creature whom He has made violated; nor is the free working of second causes put aside; rather is it established. In all these matters the divine wisdom appears, as also does God's power and faithfulness in effecting that which He has purposed.

Num. 23:19; Isa. 46:10; John 19:11; Acts 4:27,28; Rom. 9:15,18; Eph. 1: 3-5,11; Heb. 6:17; Jas. 1:13; 1 John 1:5.

2 God's decree is not based upon His foreknowledge that, under certain conditions, certain happenings will take place, but is independent of all such foreknowledge.

Acts 15:18; Rom. 9:11,13,16,18.

3 By His decree, and for the manifestation of His glory, God has predestinated (or foreordained) certain men and angels to eternal life through Jesus Christ, thus revealing His grace. Others, whom He has left to perish in their sins, show the terrors of His justice.

Matt. 25:34; Rom. 9:22,23; Eph. 1:5,6; 1 Tim. 5:21; Jude 4.

4 The angels and men who are the subjects of God's predestination are clearly and irreversibly designated, and their number is unalterably fixed.

John 13:18; 2 Tim. 2:19.

5 Before the world was made, God's eternal, immutable purpose, which originated in the secret counsel and good pleasure of His will, moved Him to choose (or to elect), in Christ, certain of mankind to everlasting glory.   Out of His mere free grace and love He predestinated these chosen ones to life, although there was nothing in them to cause Him to choose them.

Rom. 8:30; 9:13,16; Eph. 1:4,9,11; 2:5,12; 1 Thess. 5:9; 2 Tim. 1:9.

6 Not only has God appointed the elect to glory in accordance with the eternal and free purpose of His will, but He has also foreordained the means by which His purpose will be effected. Since His elect are children of Adam and therefore among those ruined by Adam's fall into sin, He willed that they should be redeemed by Christ, and effectually called to faith in Christ. Furthermore, by the working of His Spirit in due season they are justified, adopted, sanctified, and 'kept by His power through faith unto salvation'.   None but the elect partake of any of these great benefits.

John 6:64; 10:26; 17:9; Rom. 8:30; 1 Thess. 5:9,10; 2 Thess. 2:13; 1 Pet. 1:2,5.

7 The high mystery of predestination needs to be handled with special prudence and caution, so that men, being directed to the will of God revealed in His Word and obeying the same, may become assured of their eternal election through the certainty of their effectual calling.   By this means predestination will promote the praise of God, and reverential awe and wonder.   It will encourage humility and diligence, and bring much comfort to all who sincerely obey the gospel.

Luke 10:20; Rom. 11:5,6,20,33; Eph. 1:6; 1 Thess. 1:4,5; 2 Pet. 1:10.

CHAPTER 4

CREATION

1 IN the beginning it pleased the Triune God—Father, Son and Holy Spirit—to create the world and all things in it in six days. All was very good. In this way God glorified His eternal power, wisdom and goodness.

Gen. 1:31; Job 26:13; John 1:2,3; Rom. 1:20; Col. 1:16; Heb. 1:2.

2 All creatures were made by God, the last to be fashioned being man and woman who received dominion over all other creatures on the earth. God gave man and woman rational and immortal souls, and in all respects fitted them for a life in harmony with Himself. They were created in His image, possessing knowledge, righteousness and true holiness. The divine law was written in their hearts and they had power to obey it fully. Yet, being left to the liberty of their own mutable wills, transgression of the law was a possibility.

Gen. 1:26,27; 2:7; 3:6; Eccles. 7:29; Rom. 2:14,15.

3 The law of God in general was written in the hearts of the first human pair, but at the same time they were placed under a special prohibition not to eat of the tree of the knowledge of good and evil. Their happiness and fellowship with God depended upon their yielding obedience to His will, as also did the continuance of their dominion over the creatures.

Gen. 1:26,28; Gen. 2:17.

CHAPTER 5

DIVINE PROVIDENCE

1 GOD who, in infinite power and wisdom, has created all things, upholds, directs, controls and governs them, both animate and inanimate, great and small, by a providence supremely wise and holy, and in accordance with His infallible foreknowledge and the free and immutable decisions of His will. He fulfils the purposes for which He created them, so that His wisdom, power and justice, together with His infinite goodness and mercy, might be praised and glorified.

Job 38:11; Ps. 135:6; Isa. 46:10,11; Matt. 10:29-31; Eph. 1:11; Heb. 1:3.

2 Nothing happens by chance or outside the sphere of God's providence. As God is the First Cause of all events, they happen immutably and infallibly according to His foreknowledge and decree, to which they stand related. Yet by His providence God so controls them, that second causes, operating either as fixed laws, or freely, or in dependence upon other causes, play their part in bringing them about.

Gen. 8:22; Prov. 16:33; Acts 2:23.

3 Ordinarily, in His providence, God makes use of means; yet He is free to work without them, to give them efficacy above what they normally possess, and even to work contrary to them, at His pleasure.

Isa. 55:10,11; Dan. 3:27; Hos. 1:7; Acts 27:31,44; Rom. 4:19-21.

4 God's almighty power, unsearchable wisdom, and infinite goodness are so far-reaching and all-pervading, that both the fall of the first man into sin, and all other sinful actions of angels and men, proceed according to His sovereign purposes. It is not that He gives His bare permission, for in a variety of ways He wisely and powerfully limits, orders and governs sinful actions, so that they effect His holy designs. Yet the sinfulness involved in the

actions proceeds only from angels and men and not from God who, being most holy and righteous, neither is nor can be the author or approver of sin.

Gen. 1:20; 2 Sam. 24:1; 2 Kings 19:28; 1 Chron. 21:1; Ps. 50:21; 76:10; Isa. 10:6,7,12; Rom. 11:32-34; 1 John 2:16.

5 God, who is most wise, righteous and gracious, frequently allows His own people to fall for a time into a variety of temptations, and to experience the sinfulness of their own hearts. This He does in order to chastise them for sins which they have committed, or to teach them humility by revealing to them the hidden strength of evil and deceitfulness remaining in their hearts. His purpose is also to cause them to realize their need to depend fully and at all times upon Himself, and to help them to guard against sin in the future. In these and other ways His just and holy purposes are worked out, so that all that happens to His elect ones is by His appointment, for His glory, and for their good.

2 Chron. 32:25,26,31; Rom. 8:28; 2 Cor. 12:7-9.

6 God, as a righteous judge, deals otherwise with wicked and ungodly men. He awards them blindness and hardness of heart for their sins. He withholds from them the grace which might have enlightened their minds and exercised their hearts, and in some cases recalls the gifts He had bestowed upon them. Also, He sets them in situations which their evil hearts seize upon as opportunities for sin. In other words, He abandons them to their own innate corruptions, to the temptations of the world, and to the power of Satan, with the consequence that they harden themselves by the use of the very means which God employs for softening the hearts of others.

Exod. 8:15,32; Deut. 2:30; 29:4; 2 Kings 8:12,13; Ps. 81:11,12; Isa. 6:9, 10; Matt. 13:12; Rom. 1:24-26,28; 11:7,8; 2 Thess. 2:10-12; 1 Pet. 2:7,8.

7 God's general providence reaches out to all creatures, but in a very special way it is directed to the care of His church. All things are controlled providentially for the good of the church.

Isa. 43:3-5; Amos 9:8,9; 1 Tim. 4:10.

CHAPTER 6

THE FALL OF MAN:
SIN AND ITS PUNISHMENT

1 MAN, as he came from the hand of God, his creator, was upright and perfect. The righteous law which God gave him spoke of life as conditional upon his obedience, and threatened death upon his disobedience. Adam's obedience was short-lived. Satan used the subtle serpent to draw Eve into sin. Thereupon she seduced Adam who, without any compulsion from without, wilfully broke the law under which they had been created, and also God's command not to eat of the forbidden fruit. To fulfil His own wise and holy purposes God permitted this to happen, for He was directing all to His own glory.

Gen. 2:16,17; Gen. 3:12,13; 2 Cor. 11:3.

2 By this sin our first parents lost their former righteousness, and their happy communion with God was severed. Their sin involved us all, and by it death appertained to all. All men became dead in sin, and totally polluted in all parts and faculties of both soul and body.

Gen. 6:5; Jer. 17:9; Rom. 3:10-19,23; 5:12-21; Titus 1:15.

3 The family of man is rooted in the first human pair. As Adam and Eve stood in the room and stead of all mankind, the guilt of their sin was reckoned by God's appointment to the account of all their posterity, who also from birth derived from them a polluted nature. Conceived in sin and by nature children subject to God's anger, the servants of sin and the subjects of death, all men are now given up to unspeakable miseries, spiritual, temporal and eternal, unless the Lord Jesus Christ sets them free.

Job 14:4; Ps. 51:5; Rom. 5:12-19; 6:20; 1 Cor. 15:21,22,45,49; Eph. 2:3; 1 Thess. 1:10; Heb. 2:14,15.

4 The actual sins that men commit are the fruit of the corrupt nature transmitted to them by our first parents. By reason of

this corruption, all men become wholly inclined to all evil; sin disables them. They are utterly indisposed to, and, indeed, rendered opposite to, all that is good.

Matt. 15:19; Rom. 8:7; Col. 1:21; Jas. 1:14.

5 During this earthly life corrupt nature remains in those who are born of God, that is to say, regenerated. Through Christ it is pardoned and mortified, yet both the corruption itself, and all that issues from it, are truly and properly sin.

Eccles. 7:20; Rom. 7:18,23-25; Gal. 5:17; 1 John 1:8.

CHAPTER 7

GOD'S COVENANT

1 THE distance between God and His creature man is so great that, although men, endowed as they are with reason, owe obedience to Him as their creator, yet they could never have attained to life as their reward had not God, in an act of voluntary condescension, made this possible by the making of a covenant.

Job 35:7,8; Luke 17:10.

2 Furthermore, since man, by reason of his fall into sin, had brought himself under the curse of God's law, it pleased the Lord to make a covenant of grace, in which He freely offers life and salvation by Jesus Christ to sinners. On their part He requires faith in Him that they may be saved, and promises to give His Holy Spirit to all those who are elected unto eternal life, in order that they may be made willing and able to believe.

Gen. 2:17; Ps. 110:3; Ezek. 36:26,27; Mark 16:15,16; John 3:16; 6:44,45; Rom. 3:20,21; 8:3; Gal. 3:10.

3 God's covenant is revealed in the gospel; in the first place to Adam in the promise of salvation by 'the seed of the woman', and

afterwards, step by step, until the full revelation of salvation was completed in the New Testament. The salvation of the elect is based upon a covenant of redemption that was transacted in eternity between the Father and the Son; and it is solely through the grace conveyed by this covenant that all the descendants of fallen Adam who have been saved have obtained life and a blessed immortality; for the terms of blessing which applied to Adam in his state of innocency have no application to his posterity to render them acceptable to God.

Gen. 3:15; John 8:56; Acts 4:12; Rom. 4:1-5; 2 Tim. 1:9; Titus 1:2; Heb. 1:1,2; 11:6,13.

CHAPTER 8

CHRIST THE MEDIATOR

1 TO give effect to His eternal purpose God chose and ordained the Lord Jesus, His only begotten Son, in accordance with the covenant into which they had entered, to be the mediator between God and man; also to be prophet, priest, king, head and saviour of His church; also to be the heir of all things and judge of the world. From all eternity God had given to His Son those who were to be His progeny, and the Son engaged in time (as distinct from eternity) to redeem, call, justify, sanctify, and glorify them.

Ps. 2:6; Isa. 42:1; 53:10; Luke 1:33; John 17:6; Acts 3:22; 17:31; Rom. 8:30; Eph. 1:22,23; Heb. 1:2; 5:5,6; 1 Pet. 1:19,20.

2 The divine Person who made the world, and upholds and governs all things that He has made, is the Son of God, the second Person of the Holy Trinity. He is true and eternal God, the 'brightness of the Father's glory', of the same substance (or essence) as the Father, and equal with Him. It is He who, at the

appointed time, took upon Himself the nature of man, with all its essential characteristics and its common infirmities, sin excepted. He was conceived by the Holy Spirit in the womb of the Virgin Mary, a woman who belonged to the tribe of Judah, the Holy Spirit coming down upon her and the power of God most High overshadowing her. And so, as the Scripture tells us, He was made of a woman, a descendant of Abraham and David. In this way it came about that the two whole, perfect, and distinct natures, the divine and the human, were inseparably joined together in one Person, without the conversion of the one nature into the other, and without the mixing, as it were, of one nature with the other; in other words, without confusion. Thus the Son of God is now both true God and true man, yet one Christ, the only mediator between God and man.

Matt. 1:22,23; Luke 1:27,31,35; John 1:14; Rom. 8:3; 9:5; Gal. 4:4; 1 Tim. 2:5; Heb. 2:14,16,17; 4:15.

3 The two natures, divine and human, being thus united in the person of God's Son, He was sanctified and anointed with the Holy Spirit to an unlimited extent, and in Him are found all treasures of wisdom and knowledge. He is replete with all that is pleasing to the Father, being holy, harmless, untouched by sin, and full of grace and truth. Thus He has become thoroughly qualified to execute the work of a mediator and surety. He did not take this work upon Himself uncalled, but was commissioned by His Father so to act. His Father also conferred upon Him full powers of jurisdiction and commanded Him to pass judgment on all.

Ps. 45:7; Matt. 28:18; John 1:14; 3:34; 5:22,27; Acts 2:36; 10:38; Col. 1: 19; 2:3; Heb. 5:5; 7:22,26.

4 The Lord Jesus most willingly undertook the office of mediator, and in order that He might discharge it He became subject to God's law, which He perfectly fulfilled. He also underwent the punishment due to us, which we should have borne and suffered, for He bore our sins and was accursed for our sakes. He endured sorrows in His soul severe beyond our conception, and most

painful sufferings in His body. His death was by crucifixion. While He remained in the state of the dead His body sustained no decay. The third day saw His resurrection in the same body in which He had suffered. In the same body also He ascended into heaven, where He sits at the right hand of His Father, interceding for His own. At the end of the world He will return to judge men and angels.

Ps. 40:7,8; Isa. 53:6; Matt. 3:15; 26:37,38; 27:46; Mark 16:19; Luke 22: 44; John 10:18; 20:25,27; Acts 1:9-11; 10:42; 13:37; Rom. 8:34; 14:9,10; 1 Cor. 15:3,4; 2 Cor. 5:21; Gal. 3:13; 4:4; Heb. 9:24; 10:5-10; 1 Pet. 3: 18; 2 Pet. 2:4.

5 By His perfect obedience to God's law, and by a once-for-all offering up of Himself to God as a sacrifice through the eternal Spirit, the Lord Jesus has fully satisfied all the claims of divine justice. He has brought about reconciliation, and purchased an everlasting inheritance in the kingdom of heaven, for all those given to Him by His Father.

John 17:2; Rom. 3:25,26; Heb. 9:14,15.

6 The price of redemption was not actually paid by Christ until after His birth in this world, but the value, efficacy and benefits of His redemptive work availed for His elect in all ages successively from the beginning of the world. This was accomplished by the promises, the types and the sacrifices in which He was revealed, and which signified Him to be the woman's 'seed' (offspring) who should bruise the head of the serpent (the devil), also 'the Lamb slain from the foundation of the world'. As the Christ He is 'the same yesterday, and today, and for ever'.

1 Cor. 4:10; Heb. 4:2; 13:8; 1 Pet. 1:10,11; Rev. 13:8.

7 In His work as mediator between God and men, Christ acts according to His two natures, one divine, one human, in each nature doing that which is appropriate to it. Yet by reason of the unity of His Person, that which is appropriate to one nature is, in Scripture, sometimes attributed to the Person denominated by the other nature.

John 3:13; Acts 20:28.

8 Christ certainly and effectually applies and communicates eternal redemption to all those for whom He has obtained it. His work of intercession is on their behalf. He unites them to Himself by His Spirit; He reveals to them, in and by the Word, the mystery of salvation; He persuades them to believe and obey, governing their hearts by His Word and Spirit; He overcomes all their enemies by His almighty power and wisdom, using those methods and ways which are most agreeable to the wonderful and unsearchable appointments of His providence. All these things are carried out in His free and sovereign grace, and unconditionally, nothing of merit being foreseen by Him in the elect.

Ps. 110:1; John 3:8; 6:37; 10:15,16; 17:6,9; Rom. 5:10; 8:9,14; 1 Cor. 15: 25,26; Eph. 1:8,9; 1 John 5:20.

9 Christ, and Christ alone, is fitted to be mediator between God and man. He is the prophet, priest and king of the church of God. His office as mediator cannot be transferred from Him to any other, either in whole or in part.

1 Tim. 2:5.

10 Christ's threefold offices are necessary for us. Because of our ignorance we stand in need of His prophetical office; because of our estrangement from God and the imperfection of our services at their best, we need His priestly office to reconcile us to God and render us acceptable to Him; because we have turned away from God and are utterly unable to return to Him, and also because we need to be rescued and rendered secure from our spiritual adversaries, we need His kingly office to convince, subdue, draw, sustain, deliver and preserve us, until we finally enter His heavenly kingdom.

Ps. 110:3; Luke 1:74,75; John 1:18; 16:8; Gal. 5:17; Col. 1:21.

CHAPTER 9

FREE WILL

1 IN the natural order God has endued man's will with liberty and the power to act upon choice, so that it is neither forced from without, nor by any necessity arising from within itself, compelled to do good or evil.

Deut. 30:19; Matt. 17:12; Jas. 1:14.

2 In his state of innocency man had freedom and power to will and to do what was good and acceptable to God. Yet, being unstable, it was possible for him to fall from his uprightness.

Gen. 3:6; Eccles. 7:29.

3 As the consequence of his fall into a state of sin, man has lost all ability to will the performance of any of those works, spiritually good, that accompany salvation. As a natural (unspiritual) man he is dead in sin and altogether opposed to that which is good. Hence he is not able, by any strength of his own, to turn himself to God, or even to prepare himself to turn to God.

John 6:44; Rom. 5:6; 8:7; Eph. 2:1,5; Titus 3:3-5.

4 When God converts a sinner, and brings him out of sin into the state of grace, He frees him from his natural bondage to sin and, by His grace alone, He enables him freely to will and to do that which is spiritually good. Nevertheless certain corruptions remain in the sinner, so that his will is never completely and perfectly held in captivity to that which is good, but it also entertains evil.

John 8:36; Rom. 7:15,18,19,21,23; Phil. 2:13; Col. 1:13.

5 It is not until man enters the state of glory that he is made perfectly and immutably free to will that which is good, and that alone.

Eph. 4:13.

CHAPTER 10

EFFECTUAL CALLING

1 AT a time appointed by and acceptable to God, those whom God has predestinated to life are effectually called by His Word and Spirit out of the state of death in which they are by nature, to grace and salvation by Jesus Christ. Their minds are given spiritual enlightenment and, as those who are being saved, they begin to understand the things of God. God takes away their heart of stone and gives them a heart of flesh. He renews their will, and by His almighty power He sets them to seek and follow that which is good, at the same time effectually drawing them to Jesus Christ. And to all these changes they come most freely, for they are made willing by divine grace.

Deut. 30:6; Ps. 110:3; Song 1:4; Ezek. 36:26,27; Acts 26:18; Rom. 8:30; 11:7; Eph. 1:10,11,17,19; 2:1-6; 2 Thess. 2:13,14.

2 God's effectual call is the outcome of His free and special grace alone. Until a man is given life, and renewed by the Holy Spirit, he is dead in sins and trespasses, so is entirely passive in this work of salvation, a work that does not proceed from anything good foreseen in him, nor from any power or agency resident in him. The power that enables him to answer God's call and to embrace the grace offered and conveyed in it, is no less than that which effected the resurrection of Christ from the dead.

John 5:25; 1 Cor. 2:14; Eph. 1:19,20; 2:5,8; 2 Tim. 1:9.

3 Elect infants dying in infancy are regenerated and saved by Christ through the Spirit, who works when and where and how He pleases. The same is true of all elect persons who are incapable of being outwardly called through the preaching of the gospel.

John 3:3,5,6,8.

4 Men who are not elected, even though they may be called upon to embrace salvation by the preachers of the gospel, and

may be the subjects of some common operations of the Spirit, cannot be saved, because they are not effectually drawn to Christ by the Father, for which reason they neither can, nor will, truly come to Him. Much less can men who do not receive the Christian religion be saved, no matter how diligent they are to frame their lives according to the light of nature and the teachings of the religion which they follow.

Matt. 13:20,21; 22:14; John 4:22; 6:44,45,65; 17:3; Acts 4:12; Heb. 6:4-6; 1 John 2:24,25.

CHAPTER 11

JUSTIFICATION

1 GOD freely justifies the persons whom He effectually calls. He does this, not by infusing righteousness into them, but by pardoning their sins and by accounting them, and accepting them, as righteous. This He does for Christ's sake alone, and not for anything wrought in them or done by them. The righteousness which is imputed to them, that is, reckoned to their account, is neither their faith nor the act of believing nor any other obedience to the gospel which they have rendered, but Christ's obedience alone. Christ's one obedience is twofold—His active obedience rendered to the entire divine law, and His passive obedience rendered in His death. Those thus justified receive and rest by faith upon Christ's righteousness; and this faith they have, not of themselves, but as the gift of God.

John 1:12; Rom. 3:24; 4:5-8; 5:17-19; 8:30; 1 Cor. 1:30,31; Eph. 1:7; 2:8-10; Phil. 3: 8,9.

2 The faith which receives and rests on Christ and His righteousness is the sole means of justification. Yet it is never alone in the

33

person justified, but is invariably accompanied by all other saving graces. Nor is it a dead faith, for it works by love.

Rom. 3:28; Gal. 5:6; Jas. 2:17,22,26.

3 By His obedience and death Christ paid in full the debt of all those who are justified. By the sacrifice of Himself in His blood-shedding on Calvary, and His suffering on their behalf of the penalty they had incurred, He fully and absolutely satisfied all the claims which God's justice had upon them. Yet their justification is altogether of free grace, firstly because Christ was the free gift of the Father to act on their behalf; secondly because Christ's obedience and His satisfying the demands of the law was freely accepted on their behalf; and thirdly because nothing in them merited these mercies. Hence God's exact justice and His rich grace are alike rendered glorious in the justification of sinners.

Isa. 53:5,6; Rom. 3:26; 8:32; 2 Cor. 5:21; Eph. 1:6,7; 2:7; Heb. 10:14; 1 Pet. 1:18,19.

4 From all eternity God decreed to justify all the elect, and in the fulness of time Christ died for their sins and rose again for their justification. Nevertheless they are not justified personally until, in due time, the Holy Spirit actually applies to them the benefits of Christ's Person and work.

Rom. 4:25; Gal. 3:8; Col. 1:21,22; 1 Tim. 2:6; Titus 3:4-7; 1 Pet. 1:2.

5 God continues to forgive the sins of all the justified. They can never lose their justification; but they may, by reason of sin, fall under God's fatherly displeasure; in which case, until they humble themselves, confess their sins, beg God's pardon, and renew their faith and repentance, God will not usually restore to them 'the light of His countenance'.

Ps. 32:5; Ps. 51; Ps. 89:31-33; Matt. 6:12; 26:75; John 10:28; 1 John 1:7,9.

6 Believers in Old Testament times were justified in precisely the same way as New Testament believers.

Rom. 4:22-24; Gal. 3:9.

CHAPTER 12

ADOPTION

FOR the sake of His only Son, Jesus Christ, God has been pleased to make all justified persons sharers in the grace of adoption, by means of which they are numbered with, and enjoy the liberties and privileges of children of God. Furthermore, God's name is put upon them, they receive the spirit of adoption, and they are enabled to come boldly to the throne of grace and to cry 'Abba, Father'. They are pitied, protected, provided for, and chastened by God as by a Father. He never casts them off, but, as they remain sealed to the day of redemption, they inherit the promises as heirs of everlasting salvation.

Ps. 103:13; Prov. 14:26; Isa. 54:8,9; Lam. 3:31; John 1:12; Rom. 8:15,17; 2 Cor. 6:18; Gal. 4:4-6; Eph. 1:5; 2:18; 4:30; Heb. 1:14; 6:12; 12:6; 1 Pet. 5:7; Rev. 3:12.

CHAPTER 13

SANCTIFICATION

1 THOSE who are united to Christ, effectually called, and regenerated, have a new heart and a new spirit created in them; and by His Word and Spirit dwelling within them, this personal work of sanctification is indeed carried further. All these blessings accrue to them by reason of the merits of Christ's death and resurrection. Sin's mastery over them is completely broken; the evil desires to which it gives birth are increasingly weakened and dealt their death-blow; and saving graces in them are

increasingly enlivened and strengthened. The practice of all true holiness, without which no man shall see the Lord, is thus promoted.

John 17:17; Acts 20:32; Rom. 6:5,6,14; 2 Cor. 7:1; Gal. 5:24; Eph. 3: 16-19; Col. 1:11; 1 Thess. 5:21-23; Heb. 12:14.

2 Sanctification, as defined in this way, extends to every part of man, yet remains incomplete in this life. Sin's corrupt remnants continue to defile all parts of man, causing within him a continual warfare that does not admit of reconciliation; the flesh rises up against the Spirit and the Spirit against the flesh.

Rom. 7:18,23; Gal. 5:17; 1 Thess. 5:23; 1 Pet. 2:11.

3 In the war of flesh versus Spirit, sin's corrupt remnants may for a time gain the upper hand, yet the continual supply of strength from the sanctifying Spirit of Christ enables man as a new creature to gain the victory. And so the saints grow in grace, moving on towards a fulness of holiness in the fear of God. They earnestly endeavour to live according to heaven's laws, and to render gospel obedience to all the commands which Christ, as their head and king, has laid down for them in His Word.

Rom. 6:14; 7:23; 2 Cor. 3:18; 7:1; Eph. 4:15,16.

CHAPTER 14

SAVING FAITH

1 THE grace of faith by which the elect are enabled to believe to the saving of their souls is the work of the Spirit in their hearts. Normally it is brought into being through the preaching of the Word. By the Word and its ministry, by the administration of baptism and the Lord's supper, by prayer, and also by other means appointed by God, faith is increased and strengthened.

Luke 17:5; Acts 20:32; Rom. 10:14,17; 2 Cor. 4:13; Eph. 2:8; 1 Pet. 2:2.

2 By faith a Christian believes everything to be true that is made known in the Word, in which God speaks authoritatively. He also perceives in the Word a degree of excellence superior to all other writings, indeed to all things that the world contains. The Word shows the glory of God as seen in His various attributes, the excellence of Christ in His nature and in the offices He bears, and the power and perfection of the Holy Spirit in all the works in which He is engaged. In this way the Christian is enabled to trust himself implicitly to the truth thus believed, and to render service according to the different requirements of the various parts of Scripture. To the commands he yields obedience; when he hears threatenings he trembles; as for the divine promises concerning this life and that which is to come, he embraces them. But the principal acts of saving faith relate in the first instance to Christ as the believer accepts, receives and rests upon Him alone for justification, sanctification, and eternal life; and all by virtue of the covenant of grace.

Ps. 19:7-10; 119:72; Isa. 66:2; John 1:12; 15:14; Acts 15:11; 16:31; 24:14; Gal. 2:20; 2 Tim. 1:12; Heb. 11:13.

3 Saving faith has its gradations. It may be weak or strong. Yet, like all other kinds of saving grace, even at its lowest ebb it is quite different in its nature from the faith and common grace of temporary believers. In consequence, though it may be frequently attacked and weakened, it wins through to victory, developing in many Christians until they attain to full assurance through Christ, who is both the 'author and finisher of our faith'.

Matt. 6:30; Rom. 4:19,20; Eph. 6:16; Col. 2:2; Heb. 5:13,14; 6:11,12; 12: 2; 2 Pet. 1:1; 1 John 5:4,5.

CHAPTER 15

REPENTANCE UNTO LIFE AND SALVATION

1 SOME of the elect are not converted until well on in life, having continued in the state in which they were born, and having followed after all kinds of evil cravings and pleasures. Then God's effectual call reaches them and He gives them repentance leading on to life eternal.

Titus 3:2-5.

2 There is not a man on earth who does good and is without sin; and the best of men, through the power and deceitfulness of their indwelling corruptions and the strength of temptation, may commit great sins hateful to God. Because of this, in the covenant of grace God has mercifully made provision that believers who so sin and fall shall be restored, through repentance, to salvation.

Eccles. 7:20; Luke 22:31,32.

3 The repentance that leads on to salvation is a gospel grace by means of which a person who is caused by the Holy Spirit to feel the manifold evils of sin is also caused by faith in Christ to humble himself on account of sin. This humiliation is characterized by godly sorrow, a detestation of the sin, and self-loathing. It is accompanied by prayer for pardon and strength of grace, and also by a purpose and endeavour, in the power supplied by the Spirit, to conduct himself in the sight of God with the consistency of life that pleases Him.

Ps. 119:6,128; Ezek. 36:31; Zech. 12:10; Acts 11:18; 2 Cor. 7:11.

4 Because we carry about with us (as Scripture tells us) a 'body of death' biassed towards evil, repentance is to continue through the whole course of our lives. Hence it is every man's duty to

repent of each particular sin of which he is conscious, and to do so with particular care.

Luke 19:8; 1 Tim. 1:13,15.

5 In the covenant of grace God has made full provision for the preservation of believers in a state of salvation, so that, although even the smallest of sins deserves damnation, there is no sin so great that it will bring damnation to them that repent. This renders the constant preaching of repentance essential.

Isa. 1:16-18; 55:7; Rom. 6:23.

CHAPTER 16

GOOD WORKS

1 ONLY the works that God has commanded in His holy Word are to be accounted good works. Such works as men have invented out of blind zeal or upon the mere pretence of good intentions, are not good, for they lack the sanction of Holy Scripture.

Isa. 29:13; Mic. 6:8; Matt. 15:9; Heb. 13:21.

2 Works that are truly good, and which are done in obedience to God's commandments, are the fruits and evidences of a true and living faith. By means of them believers make known their thankfulness, strengthen their assurance of salvation, edify their brethren, adorn their Christian witness, and deprive their opponents of arguments against the gospel. In sum, they glorify God who has made them what they are, namely, new creatures in Christ; and as such they yield fruit that evidences holiness, eternal life being the outcome of all.

Ps. 116:12,13; Matt. 5:16; Rom. 6:22; Eph. 2:10; Phil. 1:11; 1 Tim. 6:1; Jas. 2:18,22; 1 Pet. 2:15; 2 Pet. 1:5-11; 1 John 2:3,5.

3 The ability of believers to do good works does not spring in any way from themselves, but is derived from the Spirit of Christ alone. But besides the graces which they receive from Him in the first instance, they need His further actual influence to give them the will and ability to perform the works that please Him. Yet this does not mean that, without that special influence, they are at liberty to grow careless of duty, for they must be diligent in stirring into activity the grace of God that is in them.

Isa. 64:7; John 15:4,5; 2 Cor. 3:5; Phil. 2:12,13; Heb. 6:11,12.

4 In rendering obedience to God, those believers who attain to the greatest height possible in this life are so far from performing works of supererogation (that is, beyond what God actually requires) that they fall short of much which, as their duty, they are bound to do.

Job. 9:2,3; Gal. 5:17.

5 We cannot, even by our best works, merit either the pardon of sin or the granting of eternal life at the hand of God, for those works are out of all proportion to the glory to come. And furthermore, there is infinite distance between us and God, and no works of ours can yield Him profit or act as payment for the debt of our former sins. Indeed, when we have done all that we can, we have done but our duty and remain unprofitable servants. We are also to remember that, so far as our works are good, they are produced by His Spirit. As far as they are our work they are marred, and mixed with so much weakness and imperfection that they fail utterly to meet the searching requirements of God's standards.

Ps. 143:2; Isa. 64:6; Luke 17:10; Rom. 3:20; 4:6; Gal. 5:22,23; Eph. 2:8,9.

6 Nevertheless, since believers as to their persons are accepted by God through Christ, their works also are accepted as being wrought in Christ. Not as though they were, during this life, beyond reproach and unreprovable in the sight of God, but that, as He looks upon them in His Son, He is pleased to accept and

reward that which is sincere, even though it is accompanied by many weaknesses and imperfections.

Matt. 25:21,23; Eph. 1:6; Heb. 6:10; 1 Pet. 2:5.

7 As for works done by unregenerate men, even though God may have commanded them, and they may be highly useful both to themselves and to others, yet they remain sinful works for the following reasons: they do not originate in a heart purified by faith; they are not done in the right manner prescribed in Scripture; and they are not directed to the glory of God as the only right end. Hence they cannot please God, nor can they make a man fit for the reception of grace. Yet the neglect of such works is more sinful and more displeasing to God than is the performance of them.

Gen. 4:5; 1 Kings 21:27,29; 2 Kings 10:30; Job 21:14,15; Amos 5:21,22; Matt. 6:2,5; 25:41-43; Rom. 9:16; 1 Cor. 13:1; Titus 3:5; Heb. 11:4,6.

CHAPTER 17

THE PERSEVERANCE OF THE SAINTS

1 THE saints are those whom God has accepted in Christ the Beloved, and effectually called and sanctified by His Spirit. To them He has given the precious faith that pertains to all His elect. The persons to whom such blessings have been imparted can neither totally nor finally fall from the state of grace, but they shall certainly persevere in grace to the end and be eternally saved, for God will never repent of having called them and made gifts to them. Consequently He continues to beget and to nourish in them faith, repentance, love, joy, hope, and all the graces of the Spirit that issue in immortality. Many storms and floods may arise and beat upon them, yet they can never be

moved from the foundation and rock on which by faith they are firmly established. Even if unbelief and Satan's temptations cause them for a time to lose the sight and comfort of the light and love of God, yet the unchanging God remains their God, and He will certainly keep and save them by His power until they come to the enjoyment of their purchased possession; for they are engraven on the palms of His hands, and their names have been written in the book of life from all eternity.

Ps. 89:31,32; Mal. 3:6; John 10:28,29; 1 Cor. 11:32; Phil. 1:6; 2 Tim. 2:19; 1 John 2:19.

2 It is on no free will of their own that the saints' perseverance depends, but on the immutability of the decree of election, which in its turn depends upon the free and unchangeable love of God the Father, the efficacious merit and intercession of Jesus Christ and the saints' union with Him, the oath of God, the abiding character of the Spirit's indwelling of the saints, the divine nature of which they are partakers and, lastly, the terms of the covenant of grace. All these factors guarantee the certainty and infallibility of the saints' perseverance.

Jer. 32:40; John 14:19; Rom. 5:9,10; 8:30; 9:11,16; Heb. 6:17,18; 1 John 3:9.

3 In various ways—the temptations of Satan and of the world, the striving of indwelling sin to get the upper hand, the neglect of the means appointed for their preservation—saints may fall into fearful sins, and may even continue in them for a time. In this way they incur God's displeasure, grieve His Holy Spirit, do injury to their graces, diminish their comforts, experience hardness of heart and accusations of conscience, hurt and scandalize others, and bring God's chastisements on themselves. Yet being saints their repentance will be renewed, and through faith they will be preserved in Christ Jesus to the end.

2 Sam. 12:14; Ps. 32:3,4; 51:10,12; Isa. 64:5,9; Matt. 26:70,72,74; Luke 22:32,61,62; Eph. 4:30.

CHAPTER 18

THE ASSURANCE OF GRACE
AND SALVATION

1 ALTHOUGH temporary believers and other unregenerate persons may be deceived by erroneous, self-engendered notions into thinking that they are in God's favour and in a state of salvation—false and perishable hopes indeed!—yet all who truly believe in the Lord Jesus Christ and love Him in sincerity, endeavouring to conduct themselves in all good conscience according to His will, may in this life be certainly assured that they are in a state of grace. They may rejoice in hope of the glory of God, knowing that such a hope will never put them to shame.

Job 8:13,14; Matt. 7:22,23; Rom. 5:2,5; 1 John 2:3; 3:14,18,19,21,24; 5:13.

2 The certainty of salvation enjoyed by the saints of God is not mere conjecture and probability based upon a fallible hope, but an infallible assurance of faith based upon the blood and righteousness of Christ revealed in the gospel. It also results from the inward evidences of the graces of the Holy Spirit, for to those graces God speaks promises. Then again, it is based upon the testimony of the Holy Spirit as the Spirit of adoption, for He bears His witness with our spirits that we are the children of God. Such witness results in the keeping of our hearts both humble and holy.

Rom. 8:15,16; Heb. 6:11,17-19; 2 Pet. 1:4,5,10,11; 1 John 3:1-3.

3 The infallible assurance of salvation is not an essential part of salvation, for a true believer may wait for a long time, and struggle with many difficulties, before he attains to it. It is not a matter of extraordinary revelation, for if he makes a right use of the means of grace, and is enabled by the Spirit to know the things that believers receive freely from God, he may well attain to it. It therefore becomes the duty of every one to be as diligent

as possible in making his calling and election sure. By doing this he will experience greater peace and joy in the Holy Spirit, greater love and thankfulness to God, and an increased strength and cheerfulness in dutiful obedience. These things are the natural outcome of the assurance of salvation, and they constitute strong evidence that assurance does not lead men into loose living.

Ps. 77:1-12; Ps. 88; 119:32; Isa. 50:10; Rom. 5:1,2,5; 6:1,2; 14:17; Titus 2:11,12,14; Heb. 6:11,12; 1 John 4:13.

4 True believers may find that their assurance of salvation fluctuates; sometimes more, sometimes less. They may prove neglectful in preserving it, as for example, if they give way to some particular sin that wounds their conscience and grieves the Spirit; or a strong temptation may suddenly spring upon them; or God may see fit to withdraw 'the light of His countenance' and cause darkness to envelop them, a course He sometimes takes even with those who fear His name. Yet, whatever happens, certain things inevitably remain with them—the new nature which is born of God, the life of faith, the love of Christ and the brethren, sincerity of heart and conscience of duty—and by reason of these and through the work carried on by the Spirit within them, the assurance of salvation may in due time be revived. In the meantime the same influences preserve them from utter despair.

Ps. 30:7; 31:22; 42:5,11; 51:8,12,14; 77:7,8; 116:11; Song 5:2,3,6; Lam. 3:26-31; Luke 22:32; 1 John 3:9.

CHAPTER 19

THE LAW OF GOD

1 GOD gave Adam a law, written in his heart, that required his full obedience; also one command in particular, namely, that he must not eat the fruit of the tree of knowledge of good and evil. Thereby Adam and all his posterity were bound to personal, complete, exact and perpetual obedience. God promised life upon the fulfilling, and threatened death upon the breach of the law, and endued Adam with power and ability to keep His law.

Gen. 2:16,17; Eccles. 7:29; Rom. 10:5; Gal. 3:10,12.

2 The same law that was first written in man's heart continued to be a perfect rule of righteousness after Adam fell into sin, and was given by God upon Mount Sinai in the form of ten commandments, written in two tables. The first four commandments constitute our duty towards God and the remaining six our duty to man. The ten are known as the moral law.

Deut. 10:4; Rom. 2:14,15.

3 Besides the moral law God also gave to the people of Israel ceremonial laws which served as types of things to come. They fell into two main groups. In one group were rites, partly relating to worship, which pre-figured Christ, His graces, actions, sufferings, and the blessings He procured for us. The other group contained a variety of instructions about moral duties. By divine appointment all these ceremonial laws were to be observed, but only until they were abrogated in New Testament days by Jesus Christ, the true Messiah and only law-giver, who was empowered by the Father to terminate them.

1 Cor. 5:7; Eph. 2:14,16; Col. 2:14,16,17; Heb. 10:1.

4 To the people of Israel God also gave sundry judicial laws which applied as long as they remained a nation. The principles of equity which appear in them are still valid, not because they

are found in Moses' laws but in virtue of their unchanging character.

1 Cor. 9:8-10.

5 Obedience to the moral law remains for ever binding upon both justified persons and all others, and that in respect of the actual content of the law, and also of the authority of God, the creator, who is its author. In the gospel Christ in no way cancels the necessity for this obedience; on the contrary He greatly stresses our obligation to obey the moral law.

Matt. 5:17-19; Rom. 3:31; 13:8-10; Jas. 2:8,10-12.

6 So far as the law is a covenant of works under which justification or condemnation is awarded, it has no application to true believers. Yet in certain other ways it is of great use to them as well as to others, for as a rule of life it informs them of the will of God and instructs them in their duty. This done, it directs and binds them to obey it. It also reveals to them the sinful defilement of their natures, their hearts and their lives, so that as they examine themselves by the light of the law, they may be convicted more deeply of sin, and caused to humble themselves on account of it and to hate it the more. At the same time the law also gives them a clearer sight of their need of Christ, and the perfection of Christ's own obedience to the law. Similarly, as the law forbids sin, it causes the regenerate to fight against the evil inclinations to sin that they find in themselves. Furthermore, the threatenings of the law are of value in showing the regenerate what their sins deserve, and what afflictions their own disobedience may cause them in this life, even while they stand delivered from the curse and the unrestricted rigour of the law. In similar manner the promises attached to the law intimate God's approbation of obedience and set forth the blessings which flow from the fulfilment of the law, but with the proviso that those blessings do not accrue to men from the law viewed as a covenant of works. The fact that a man does good and refrains from evil because the law encourages the former and deters from the latter,

is no evidence that the man is under the law and not under grace.

Rom. 3:20; 6:12-14; 7:7; 8:1; 10:4; Gal. 2:16; 1 Pet. 3:8-13.

7 The aforementioned uses of the law of God do not run contrary to the grace of the gospel, but are most happily in line with it, for the Spirit of Christ subdues the will of man and enables it to do freely and with cheerfulness that which the will of God, as revealed in the law, requires to be done.

Ezek. 36:27; Gal. 3:21.

CHAPTER 20

THE GOSPEL AND ITS GRACIOUS EXTENT

1 AS the covenant of works was broken by man's sin and was unable to confer life, God in His mercy promised to send Christ, who would be woman-born; and by means of the promise the elect would be called, and faith and repentance wrought in their hearts. In this promise the very substance of the gospel was revealed as the effectual means for the conversion and salvation of sinners.

Gen. 3:15; Rev. 7:9.

2 This promise of Christ and of salvation by Him is revealed to men by the Word of God alone. Neither the works of creation and providence, nor the light of nature, reveal Christ and His grace to men, not even in a general or obscure way; much less is it possible by their means for men who lack the revelation of Christ by the promise of the gospel to attain to saving faith or repentance.

Prov. 29:18; Isa. 25:7; 60:2,3; Rom. 1:17; 10:14,15,17.

3 The revelation of the gospel to sinners, both to nations and to certain persons, together with the promises and precepts which

belong to gospel obedience, has been made at various times and in a variety of places, according to the sovereign will and good pleasure of God. The promise of the making known of the gospel has not been made contingent upon any good use made by men of their native abilities developed by means of light common to all, for such a development has never taken place, nor can it do so. Hence in all ages the extent to which the gospel has been proclaimed, whether to wider or more confined areas, has been granted to persons and nations in greatly varying measures according to the all-wise will of God.

Ps. 147:20; Acts 16:7; Rom. 1:18-32.

4 The gospel is the only external means of making Christ and saving grace known to men, and it is completely adequate for this purpose. But that men who are dead in their sins may be born again—that is to say, made alive, or regenerated—something further is essential, namely, an effectual, invincible work of the Holy Spirit upon every part of the soul of man, whereby a new spiritual life is produced. Nothing less than such a work will bring about conversion to God.

Ps. 110:3; John 6:44; 1 Cor. 2:14; 2 Cor. 4:4,6; Eph. 1:19,20.

CHAPTER 21

CHRISTIAN LIBERTY AND LIBERTY OF CONSCIENCE

1 CHRIST has purchased for all believers a liberty inherent in the gospel. It comprises freedom from the guilt of sin, from the condemnation that follows upon guilt, from the wrath of God, and from the severity and curse of God's law. It also includes deliverance from this present evil world, and from all such things as bondage to Satan, sin's domination, the hurtfulness of afflic-

tions, the fear and sting of death, the victory of the grave, and
eternal damnation. Furthermore, it includes free access to God
and the yielding of obedience to Him, not as it were with the fear
of a slave for his master, but with a childlike love and readiness.

All these blessings were more or less enjoyed by believers in
Old Testament days, but under New Testament conditions
Christian liberty becomes more extensive. It includes freedom
from the burdens imposed by the ceremonial law to which the
Jewish church was subjected, greater boldness in approaching to
the throne of grace, and a larger measure of the free Spirit of God
than was normally granted to saints in the pre-Christian era.

Luke 1:73-75; John 7:38,39; Acts 26:18; Rom. 8:3,15,28; 1 Cor. 15:54-
57; Gal. 1:4; 3:9,13,14; 2 Thess. 1:10; Heb. 10:19-21; 1 John 4:18.

2 God alone is Lord of the conscience. He has set it free from
all obligation to receive or obey any such doctrines or demands
of men as are in any respect in opposition to His Word or not
contained in it. Indeed, to believe and obey such doctrines and
demands is tantamount to a betrayal of true liberty of conscience.
It is against all reason, and nothing less than the destruction of
liberty of conscience, when men demand of their fellows an
implicit faith, in other words, an absolute and blind obedience.

Matt. 15:9; Acts 4:19,29; Rom. 14:4; 1 Cor. 3:5; 7:23; 2 Cor. 1:24; Col.
2:20,22,23; Jas. 4:12.

3 To practise any sin, or harbour sin's evil desires, on a pretence
of enjoying Christian liberty, perverts the main purpose of gospel
grace, and imperils those guilty of such an offence, for thereby
they destroy the very purpose of Christian liberty, namely, that
the Lord's people, 'being delivered out of the hand of their
enemies, might serve Him without fear, in holiness and righteousness before Him all their days'.

Luke 1:74,75; Rom. 6:1,2; Gal. 5:13; 2 Pet. 2:18,21.

CHAPTER 22

RELIGIOUS WORSHIP, AND THE LORD'S DAY

1 THE light of nature shows that there is a God who has dominion and sovereignty over all. He is just and good, and He does good to all. He is therefore to be feared, loved, praised, invoked, trusted and served by men with all their heart and soul and strength. But the only acceptable way of worshipping the true God is appointed by Himself, in accordance with His own will. Consequently He may not be worshipped in ways of mere human contrivance, or proceeding from Satan's suggestions. Visible symbols of God, and all other forms of worship not prescribed in the Holy Scripture, are expressly forbidden.

Exod. 20:4-6; Deut. 12:32; Jer. 10:7; Mark 12:33.

2 Religious worship is to be given to God the Father, Son, and Holy Spirit, and to Him alone. It is not to be given to angels, saints, or any other creatures. Since man's fall into sin, worship cannot be rendered to God without a mediator; and the only accepted mediation is that of Christ.

Matt. 4:9,10; 28:19; John 5:23; 14:6; Rom. 1:25; Col. 2:18; 1 Tim. 2:5; Rev. 19:10.

3 God requires all men to pray to Him, and to give thanks, this being one part of natural worship. But to render such prayer acceptable, several things are requisite: it must be made in the name of God's Son, it must be Spirit-aided, and it must accord with the will of God. It must also be reverent, humble, fervent and persevering, and linked with faith, love and understanding. United prayer, when offered, must always be in a known language.

Ps. 65:2; 95:1-7; John 14:13,14; Rom. 8:26; 1 Cor. 14:16,17; 1 John 5:14.

4 Prayer is to be made for things lawful, and for men of all sorts now living or as yet unborn. But prayer is not to be made for

the dead, nor for those who are known to be guilty of 'the sin unto death'.

2 Sam. 7:29; 12:21-23; 1 Tim. 2:1,2; 1 John 5:16.

5 The reading of the Scripture, the preaching and hearing of the Word of God, the instructing and admonishing of one another by means of psalms and hymns and spiritual songs, singing with heartfelt thankfulness to the Lord, the observance of baptism and the Lord's supper—these are all parts of divine worship to be performed obediently, intelligently, faithfully, reverently, and with godly fear. Moreover, on special occasions, solemn humiliation, fastings, and thanksgivings ought to be observed in a holy and reverential manner.

Exod. 15:1-19; Esther 4:16; Ps. 107; Joel 2:12; Matt. 28:19,20; Luke 8:18; 1 Cor. 11:26; Eph. 5:19; Col. 3:16; 1 Tim. 4:13; 2 Tim. 4:2.

6 In present gospel days neither prayer nor any other aspect of religious worship depends for its efficacy on the place where it is performed or towards which it is directed, for God is everywhere to be worshipped in spirit and in truth; as, for instance, in the daily worship carried on in private families, in the worship in which individual Christians engage in secret, and in the worship of the public assemblies. Such assemblies are convened in accordance with God's Word and providence, and believers must neither carelessly neglect them nor wilfully forsake them.

Ps. 55:17; Mal. 1:11; Matt. 6:6; John 4:21; Acts 2:42; 10:2; 1 Tim. 2:8; Heb. 10:25.

7 As it is a law of nature, applicable to all, that a proportion of time, determined by God, should be allocated for the worship of God, so, by His Word, He has particularly appointed one day in seven to be kept as a holy sabbath to Himself. The commandment to this effect is positive, moral, and of perpetual application. It is binding upon all men in all ages. From the beginning of the world to the resurrection of Christ the sabbath was the last day of the week, but when Christ's resurrection took place it was changed to the first day of the week, which is called the Lord's

day. It is to be continued to the world's end as the Christian sabbath, the observance of the seventh day being abolished.

Exod. 20:8; Acts 20:7; 1 Cor. 16:1,2; Rev. 1:10.

8 Men keep the sabbath holy to the Lord when, having duly prepared their hearts and settled their mundane affairs beforehand, for the sake of the Lord's command they set aside all works, words and thoughts that pertain to their worldly employment and recreations, and devote the whole of the Lord's day to the public and private exercises of God's worship, and to duties of necessity and mercy.

Neh. 13:15-22; Isa. 58:13; Matt. 12:1-13.

CHAPTER 23

LAWFUL OATHS AND VOWS

1 A LAWFUL oath is an aspect of religious worship in which the swearer, having God's truth, justice and righteousness in view, solemnly calls God to witness what he swears, and to judge him according to the truth or falsity of his words.

Exod. 20:7; Deut. 10:20; 2 Chron. 6:22,23; Jer. 4:2.

2 An oath is only lawful when it is taken in the name of God, with all holy fear and reverence. To swear vainly or rashly by that glorious and dread name, or to swear at all by any other thing, is sinful and to be abhorred. God's Word sanctions the taking of an oath when weighty and momentous matters are engaging attention, and when truth requires confirmation and an end to strife is desired. In such circumstances it is permissible to take a lawful oath imposed by lawful authority.

Neh. 13:25; Matt. 5:34,37; 2 Cor. 1:23; Heb. 6:16; Jas. 5:12.

3 Each and every person who takes an oath agreeably to the Word of God must well consider the seriousness of such a solemn act, and be extremely careful to assert nothing but what he knows to be truth; for by rash, false and empty oaths the Lord is provoked, and by reason of them a land is brought to misery.

Lev. 19:12; Jer. 23:10.

4 An oath is to be taken in the plain and usual sense of the words used, without equivocation or mental reservation.

Ps. 24:4.

5 Vows are to be made to God alone and not to any creature. Once made they are to be performed scrupulously and faithfully. But monastical vows of perpetual single life, professed poverty, and regular obedience, that pertain to the church of Rome, so far from representing superior sanctity, are merely superstitious and sinful snares in which no Christian ought to entangle himself.

Gen. 28:20-22; Ps. 76:11; Matt. 19:11; 1 Cor. 7:2,9; Eph. 4:28.

CHAPTER 24

CIVIL GOVERNMENT

1 AS the world's supreme Lord and King, God has instituted civil government and has set up civil authorities, subject to Himself, to rule over communities for His own glory and the public good. For these purposes to be achieved He has given them the powers of life and death, both for the safety and encouragement of all men of good behaviour, and for the punishment of the wicked.

Rom. 13:1-4.

2 It is lawful for Christians to accept and carry out the duties of public office when called upon to do so, in which case it becomes their responsibility to maintain justice and peace in accordance with the sound laws of the kingdoms and states which they serve. New Testament teaching authorizes them to wage war when this is found to be just and necessary.

2 Sam. 23:3; Ps. 82:3,4; Luke 3:14.

3 As civil rulers are set up by God for the aforesaid purposes, Christians are to be subject to them in respect of all their lawful requirements, and that, for the Lord's sake and for conscience' sake, and not merely to avoid punishment. They should offer supplications and prayers for kings and all that are in authority, that under their rule they may live a 'quiet and peaceable life in all godliness and honesty'.

Rom. 13:5-7; 1 Tim. 2:1,2; 1 Pet. 2:17.

CHAPTER 25

MARRIAGE

1 MARRIAGE is to be between one man and one woman. It is not lawful for any man to have more than one wife, nor for any woman to have more than one husband, at one and the same time.

Gen. 2:24; Mal. 2:15; Matt. 19:5,6.

2 God instituted marriage for the mutual help of husband and wife, for the increase of mankind in accordance with His laws, and for the prevention of immorality.

Gen. 1:28; 2:18; 1 Cor. 7:2,9.

3 It is lawful for all sorts of people to marry, provided that they are able to give their rational consent. But it is the duty of

Christians to marry only 'in the Lord'. In consequence, those who profess the Christian faith should not contract marriages with infidels or idolaters. It is also quite unfitting for godly persons to become partners in marriage with persons who lead wicked lives or who maintain damnable heresies.

Neh. 13:25-27; 1 Cor. 7:39; 1 Tim. 4:3; Heb. 13:4.

4 Marriage must not be contracted within the degrees of blood relationship or kinship forbidden in God's Word. Nor when such incestuous unions occur can they ever be made lawful, either by any law of man or by the consenting parties, and the persons concerned can never rightly live together as man and wife.

Lev. 18; Mark 6:18; 1 Cor. 5:1.

CHAPTER 26

THE CHURCH

1 THE catholic or universal church is invisible in respect of the internal work of the Spirit and truth of grace. It consists of the whole number of the elect who have been, who are being, or who yet shall be gathered into one under Christ who is the church's head. The church is the wife, the body, the fulness of Christ, who 'fills all in all'.

Eph. 1:10,22,23; 5:23,27,32; Col. 1:18; Heb. 12:23.

2 All persons throughout the world who profess to believe the gospel and to render gospel obedience unto God by Christ are, and may be called, visible saints, provided that they do not render void their profession of belief by holding fundamental errors or by living unholy lives; and of such persons all local churches should be composed.

Acts 11:26; Rom. 1:7; 1 Cor. 1:2; Eph. 1:20-22.

3 The purest churches under heaven are liable to be troubled by mixture and error, and some have so far degenerated as no longer to be churches of Christ at all, but 'synagogues of Satan'. Nevertheless, Christ always has had a kingdom in this world of such as believe in Him and profess His name, and He ever will have such a kingdom to the world's end.

Ps. 72:17; 102:28; Matt. 16:18; 1 Cor. 5; 2 Thess. 2:11,12; Rev. 2; 3; 12: 17; 18:2.

4 The Lord Jesus Christ is the head of the church. By the appointment of the Father, all authority requisite for the calling, establishment, ordering and governing of the church is supremely and sovereignly invested in Him. It is impossible for the Pope of Rome in any true sense to be the head of the church, for he is the antichrist, described in Scripture as 'the man of sin', 'the son of perdition,' who 'exalts himself' in the church against Christ and 'above all that is called God', whom 'the Lord shall destroy with the brightness of His coming'.

Matt. 28:18-20; Eph. 4:11,12; Col. 1:18; 2 Thess. 2:2-9.

5 In the exercise of the authority which has been entrusted to Him, the Lord Jesus, through the ministry of the Word and by His Spirit, calls to Himself out of the world those who are given to Him by His Father, that they may live in His sight, rendering Him the obedience prescribed by Him for them in the Scripture. He commands those thus called to form particular societies or churches to promote their common welfare, and to engage in the public worship which He requires them to carry on while they continue in the world.

Matt. 18:15-20; 28:20; John 10:16; 12:32.

6 The members of these churches are saints by reason of the divine call, and in a visible manner they demonstrate and declare, both by their confession of Christ and their manner of life, that they obey Christ's call. They willingly consent to hold fellowship together according to Christ's instructions, giving themselves

to the Lord and to one another as God wills, and yielding full assent to the requirements of the gospel.

Acts 2:41,42; 5:13,14; Rom. 1:7; 1 Cor. 1:2; 2 Cor. 9:13.

7 To each of these churches thus gathered according to the divine will made known in His Word, the Lord has given all the power and authority requisite for the carrying on of the form of worship and discipline which He has appointed for their observance. This extends to the provision of such commands and rules as are needful for the rightful and proper use of the power conferred on the churches.

Matt. 18:17,18; 1 Cor. 5:4,5; 5:13; 2 Cor. 2:6-8.

8 A local church, gathered and fully organized according to the mind of Christ, consists of officers and members. By Christ's appointment the officers to be chosen and set apart by the church as called and gathered, are bishops (otherwise called elders) and deacons. It is their special responsibility to arrange for the carrying out of what the Lord has ordained, and to use the powers entrusted to them for the execution of their duties; and such arrangements are to continue in the church until the world ends.

Acts 20:17,28; Phil. 1:1.

9 By Christ's appointment, any person who has been qualified and given the necessary gifts by the Holy Spirit for the work of bishop or elder in a church, must be chosen and called to that office by the common suffrage of the church itself. He must be solemnly set apart by fasting and prayer, with the laying on of the hands of the existing eldership, if there be such. Similarly, deacons are to be chosen by the common suffrage of the church, and set apart by prayer and the laying on of hands.

Acts 6:3,5,6; 14:23; 1 Tim. 4:14.

10 Pastors are required to give constant attention to the service of Christ in His churches; they are to be engaged in the ministry of the Word and in prayer, and to seek the welfare of men's souls as those that must give account to the Lord. It is therefore

imperative that the churches to which they minister should give them, according to the churches' ability, not only all due honour, but such abundance of this world's material good as will enable them to live in comfort, without the need to entangle themselves in secular employment, and which will also suffice to enable them to exercise hospitality towards others. Such an arrangement is required by the law of nature itself, and by the express command of our Lord Jesus, who has decreed that 'they that preach the gospel should live of the gospel'.

Acts 6:4; 1 Cor. 9:6-14; Gal. 6:6,7; 1 Tim. 3:2; 5:17,18; 2 Tim. 2:4; Heb. 13:17.

11 Although it is the duty of the elders or pastors of the churches, according to their office, to be constantly active in preaching the Word, yet such a work is not to be regarded as confined wholly to them, for the Holy Spirit may qualify others for the same work by giving them the necessary gifts. In this case, when such men are approved and called to the work by the church, they may and ought to perform it.

Acts 11:19-21; 1 Pet. 4:10,11.

12 All believers are under obligation to join themselves to local churches when and where they have opportunity to do so. It follows that all who are admitted to the privileges of church fellowship also become subject to the discipline and government of the church in accordance with the rule of Christ.

1 Thess. 5:14; 2 Thess. 3:6,14,15.

13 Any church members who have taken offence at the behaviour towards them of other church members, and who have obeyed the instructions laid down in Scripture for dealing with such cases, must refrain from disturbing the peace of the church, nor should they absent themselves from church assemblies or the administration of church ordinances on account of their being offended by certain of their fellow-members; but they must wait upon Christ in the further proceedings of the church.

Matt. 18:15-17; Eph. 4:2,3.

14 All members of each local church are engaged to pray continually for the good and the prosperity of all churches of Christ, wherever located, and upon all occasions to assist all other believers, within the limits of their own areas and callings, in the exercise of their gifts and graces. It follows, therefore, that churches should seek fellowship one with another, so far as the providence of God provides opportunity for the enjoyment of such benefits.

Ps. 122:6; Rom. 16:1,2; Eph. 6:18; 3 John 8-10.

15 When difficulties or differences occur in respect of doctrine or church government, and peace, unity and edification are at risk, one church only may be involved, or the churches in general may be concerned. Again, a member or members of a church may be injured by disciplinary proceedings not agreeable to truth and church order. In such cases as these it is according to the mind of Christ that many churches in fellowship together should meet and confer together through their chosen representatives, who are able to give their advice on the matters in dispute to all the churches concerned. It must be understood, however, that the representatives assembled are not entrusted with any church power properly so called, nor have they any jurisdiction over the churches themselves to exercise discipline upon any churches or persons, or to impose their conclusions on the churches or their officers.

Acts 15:2,4,6,22,23,25; 2 Cor. 1:24; 1 John 4:1.

CHAPTER 27

THE FELLOWSHIP OF SAINTS

1 ALL saints are united to Jesus Christ their head by His Spirit and by faith. But this does not mean that they become one person with Him. Yet they have fellowship in His graces, sufferings, death, resurrection, and glory. Also, as they are united to one another in love, they enjoy fellowship in the gifts and graces one of another, and are under obligation to render such services, public and private, as promote their mutual well-being, in both spiritual and temporal matters.

John 1:16; Rom. 1:12; 6:5,6; 1 Cor. 3:21-23; 12:7; Gal. 6:10; Eph. 4:15, 16; Phil. 3:10; 1 Thess. 5:11,14; 1 John 1:3; 3:17,18.

2 By their profession of faith, saints are committed to the maintenance of a holy fellowship and communion in the worship of God and in the performance of such other special services as promote their mutual well-being. They are also bound to relieve one another in their temporal concerns according to their various needs and abilities. According to the rule of the gospel, this type of fellowship, while it particularly applies to the family and church relationships of saints, is to be extended, as God gives opportunity, to the whole household of faith, that is to say, to all who in every place call upon the name of the Lord Jesus. At the same time, however, it must be understood that such a sharing one with another as saints, does not deprive any man of the title and proprietorship which he has in his own goods and possessions, nor does it infringe such title.

Acts 5:4; 11:29,30; 1 Cor. 12:14-27; Eph. 4:28; 6:4; Heb. 3:12,13; 10:24,25.

CHAPTER 28

BAPTISM AND THE LORD'S SUPPER

1 BAPTISM and the Lord's supper are ordinances which have been explicitly and sovereignly instituted by the Lord Jesus, the only lawgiver, who has appointed that they are to be continued in his church to the end of the world.

Matt. 28:19,20; 1 Cor. 11:26.

2 These holy ordinances are to be administered by those alone who are qualified and called to do so, according to the commission of Christ.

Matt. 28:19; 1 Cor. 4:1.

CHAPTER 29

BAPTISM

1 BAPTISM is an ordinance of the New Testament instituted by Jesus Christ. It is intended to be, to the person baptized, a sign of his fellowship with Christ in His death and resurrection, and of his being engrafted into Christ, and of the remission of sins. It also indicates that the baptized person has given himself up to God, through Jesus Christ, so that he may live and conduct himself 'in newness of life'.

Mark 1:4; Acts 22:16; Rom. 6:3-5; Gal. 3:27; Col. 2:12.

2 The only persons who can rightly submit themselves to this ordinance are those who actually profess repentance towards God and faith in our Lord Jesus Christ, being willing to yield obedience to Him.

Mark 16:16; Acts 2:41; 8:12,36,37; 18:8.

3 The outward element to be used in this ordinance is water, in which the believer is to be baptized in the name of the Father, and of the Son, and of the Holy Spirit.

Matt. 28:19,20; Acts 8:38.

4 Immersion, that is to say, the dipping of the believer in water, is essential for the due administration of this ordinance.

Matt. 3:16; John 3:23.

CHAPTER 30

THE LORD'S SUPPER

1 THE Lord's supper was instituted by the Lord on the same night in which He was betrayed. It is to be observed in His churches to the world's end, for a perpetual remembrance of Him and to show forth the sacrifice of Himself in His death. It was instituted also to confirm saints in the belief that all the benefits stemming from Christ's sacrifice belong to them. Furthermore, it is meant to promote their spiritual nourishment and growth in Christ, and to strengthen the ties that bind them to all the duties they owe to Him. The Lord's supper is also a bond and pledge of the fellowship which believers have with Christ and with one another.

1 Cor. 10:16,17,21; 1 Cor. 11:23-26.

2 In this ordinance Christ is not offered up to His Father, nor is any real sacrifice made in any sense of that term for remission of sin of the living or the dead. The supper is only a memorial of the one offering up of Christ, by Himself, upon the cross, once for all. It is also a spiritual offering up of all possible praise to God for the once-for-all work of Calvary. Hence the popish sacrifice of the mass, as it is called, is utterly abominable, and

injurious to Christ's own sacrifice which is the sole propitiation for all the sins of the elect.

Matt. 26:26-28; 1 Cor. 11:24; Heb. 9:25,26,28.

3   In this ordinance the Lord Jesus has directed his ministers to pray, and to bless the elements of bread and wine, and in this way to set them apart from a common to a holy use.   They are to take and break the bread, then to take the cup, and to give both to the communicants, they themselves at the same time participating in the communion.

1 Cor. 11:23-26.

4   The denial of the cup to the people, the worshipping of the elements, the lifting up of the elements, the carrying of them about for the purpose of adoration, and the reserving of them for any pretended religious use, are all contrary to the nature of the ordinance and to Christ's intention in appointing it.

Exod. 20:4,5;   Matt. 15:9; 26:26-28.

5   The outward elements in the Lord's supper—bread and wine —duly set apart for the use appointed by Christ, bear such a relation to the Lord crucified that, in a true sense although in terms used figuratively, they are sometimes called by the names of the things they represent, namely, the body and blood of Christ, even though, in substance and nature, they still remain truly and only bread and wine, as they were before being set apart for their special use.

1 Cor. 11:26-28.

6   The doctrine commonly called transubstantiation which maintains that in the supper the substance of bread and wine is changed into the substance of Christ's body and blood through consecration by a priest or in any other way, is repugnant not to Scripture alone, but even to common sense and reason.   Furthermore, it overthrows the nature of the ordinance, and has been, and is, the cause of all kinds of superstitions and gross idolatries.

Luke 24:6,39; Acts 3:21; 1 Cor. 11:24,25.

7 Those who, as worthy participants, outwardly eat and drink the visible bread and wine in this ordinance, at the same time receive and feed upon Christ crucified, and receive all the benefits accruing from His death.   This they do really and indeed, not as if feeding upon the actual flesh and blood of a person's body, but inwardly and by faith.   In the supper the body and blood of Christ are present to the faith of believers, not in any actual physical way, but in a way of spiritual apprehension, just as the bread and wine themselves are present to their outward physical senses.

1 Cor. 10:16; 11:23-26.

8 All persons who participate at the Lord's table unworthily sin against the body and blood of the Lord, and their eating and drinking brings them under divine judgment.   It follows, therefore, that all ignorant and ungodly persons, being unfit to enjoy fellowship with Christ, are similarly unworthy to be communicants at the Lord's table; and while they remain as they are they cannot rightly be admitted to partake of Christ's holy ordinance, for thereby great sin against Christ would be committed.

Matt. 7:6; 1 Cor. 11:29; 2 Cor. 6:14,15.

CHAPTER 31

THE STATE OF MAN AFTER DEATH AND THE RESURRECTION OF THE DEAD

1 THE bodies of men after death return to dust and suffer decay, but their souls which neither die nor sink into a state of unconsciousness—they are inherently immortal—immediately return to God who gave them.   The souls of the righteous, whose holiness is at death perfected, are received into paradise, where

they are with Christ, looking upon the face of God in light and glory, and waiting for the full redemption of their bodies. The souls of the wicked are cast into hell, where they remain in torment and utter darkness, reserved to the judgment of the great day. Souls separated from their bodies are in either paradise or hell, for the Scripture speaks of no other abodes of the departed.

Gen. 3:19; Eccles. 12:7; Luke 16:23,24; 23:43; Acts 13:36; 2 Cor. 5:1,6, 8; Phil. 1:23; Heb. 12:23; 1 Pet. 3:19; Jude 6,7.

2 At the last day, saints then alive on the earth will not die, but be changed. All the dead will be raised up with their selfsame bodies, and none other, although with different qualities, and shall be united again to their souls for ever.

Job 19:26,27; 1 Cor. 15:42,43,51,52; 1 Thess. 4:17.

3 By the power of Christ, the bodies of the unrighteous will be raised to dishonour. By His Spirit, Christ will raise the bodies of the righteous to honour, for they will be refashioned after the pattern of His own glorious body.

John 5:28,29; Acts 24:15; Phil. 3:21.

CHAPTER 32

THE LAST JUDGMENT

1 GOD has appointed a day in which He will judge the world in righteousness by Jesus Christ, to whom the Father has given all authority and power to judge. At that day the apostate angels will be judged. So too will all persons who have lived upon the earth; they will appear before Christ's judgment throne to give an account of their thoughts, words and deeds, and to receive His award in accordance with what they have done in this earthly life, whether good or evil.

Eccles. 12:14; Matt. 12:36; 25:32-46; John 5:22,27; Acts 17:31; Rom. 14: 10,12; 1 Cor. 6:3; 2 Cor. 5:10; Jude 6.

2   God's purpose in appointing a day of judgment is to make known the glory of His mercy in the eternal salvation of the elect, and the glory of His justice in the eternal damnation of the reprobate, that is to say, the wicked and disobedient.   In that day the righteous will inherit everlasting life, and receive a fulness of joy and glory in the Lord's presence as their eternal reward. But the wicked, who do not know God and who do not obey the gospel of Jesus Christ, will be relegated to everlasting torments and 'punished with everlasting destruction from the presence of the Lord and from the glory of His power'.

Matt. 25:21,34,46; Mark 9:48; Rom. 9:22,23; 2 Thess. 1:7-10; 2 Tim. 4:8.

3   To deter all men from sin on the one hand, and to give greater comfort to the godly in their adversity on the other, Christ would have us firmly persuaded that a day of judgment lies ahead.   For the same reasons He has kept the day's date a secret so that men may shake off all confidence in themselves and, in ignorance of the hour in which the Lord will come, may be ever on the watch, and ever prepared to say,

'Come, Lord Jesus; come quickly.   Amen.'

Mark 13:35-37; Luke 12:35-40; 2 Cor. 5:10,11; 2 Thess. 1:5-7; Rev. 22:20